EX-FREE

9 Keys To Freedom After Heartbreak

ISBN 10:   0-9801763-0-1
ISBN-13:   978-0-9801763-0-8

© Logos, Images courtesy of TROY BYER
Editors: ILANA SPECTOR, FRANK MATCHA
Cover Art: TROY BYER
Illustrations: KEATON ROGERS
Cover Design AND Layout: ROSELLE KIPP
For questions, e-mail <info@TroyByer.com>

9 8 7 6 5 4 3 2 1

Published in the United States of America by Lightning Source, Inc

EX-FREE

9 Keys To Freedom After Heartbreak

BY

Troy Byer

Foreword by
Michael Bernard Beckwith

TABLE OF CONTENTS

Foreword

In inspiring and uplifting terms, Troy offers her readers a time-tested 9-Key formula that she has successfully applied in her own life for releasing painful wounds that result from the loss of a love relationship. Her compassionate and wise approach will teach you how to gracefully move into the future fully open to its infinite possibilities, equipped with the inner freedom to embrace them.

The beauty of Troy's 9-Key formula is that it does not deny the pain that accompanies the loss of a love. In fact, her method encourages its practitioners to turn pain into an ally by using it to accurately gauge the degree of pain as well as the degree of healing as it progresses. You will be put in touch with the empowered part of yourself that invites you to become a more loving and realistic person in all of your relationships, and especially with yourself.

Brimming with practical practices, you will learn how to recognize, reframe, gently access and release deep layers of emotional holding.

This practice is vital to the fulfillment of your desire to live a new, vibrant life because unaddressed hurts continue to draw into your magnetic field people and circumstances that create similar painful lessons so that a transformative healing may be set into motion in your life.

When Troy first began attending classes at the Agape International Spiritual Center in Los Angeles, I instantly recognized her wonderful spirit and commitment to practicing the universal wisdom teachings of the ages. Drawing on her experience with various spiritual practices, Troy lovingly walks her readers through the doorway of awareness to the joys and wealth of recognizing and experiencing healthy, meaningful, mature relationships.

Wise are those who look to an experienced guide who compassionately yet firmly offers the wisdom of their own journey for releasing, healing and transforming their lives. You hold in your hands just such a book, because its author walks her talk. Read, practice, heal and transform, because all that you need to do so has always been and always will be right within you, and Troy's 9-Keys To Freedom will activate that potential.

Michael Bernard Beckwith
Founder and Spiritual Director,
The Agape International Spiritual Center

Introduction

The brains of people deeply in love do not look like those of people experiencing strong emotions, but instead like those of people snorting cocaine. Love, in other words, uses the neural mechanisms that are activated during the process of addiction.
-- Dr. Young of Rutgers University

Although I am grateful for science's newfound recognition of love, I didn't have to wait for science to confirm that as a force, love embodies the power of the world's most addictive drug. My mother's numerous marriages and eight kids from eight different men were all the evidence I needed. As a young girl, it both troubled and saddened me to watch my mother get strung out on one relationship after another.

At that time, I was certain my mother was addicted to love and like any child presumably being raised by an addict, I wanted to help her, I wanted her to stop obsessing about her exes until she pretty much married the next man she met. My wants were no match for my mother's needs. By age eleven, due to my mother's revolving door of men, coupled with a few other neglectful issues, I became a ward of the state. After living in two foster homes, I moved in with a man that neither my mother nor I had heard from or seen in ten years. He was my mother's first husband. He was the ex that truly broke my mother's heart. He was my father.

Moving in with my father, his wife and my two half brothers was a real culture shock for me. For starters, they were a normal family. They took care of each other. They genuinely loved each other. They ate meals together and although I sat beside my new family at every meal, I never felt like I belonged with them. Their family bond had been established long before I arrived and as a result, at best, I felt like a long-term visitor. Witnessing my father's family and their unity made me even angrier with my mother. As I watched my father lovingly interact with his current and seemingly perfect wife, I harshly judged my mother and her inability to get over my father the way he had clearly gotten over her.

I resented my welfare-recipient mother for not providing a similar family structure for me and my siblings. Most of all, I was angry at her for giving me a front row view of the life I would never want for me - hers. Living with my father was no walk in the park and as I grew into a young woman, I missed and needed my mother more and more. The more I missed and needed my mom, the angrier I grew.

INTRODUCTION

At night I often prayed that God would help me understand why my mother had allowed all her exes to send her life into such a downward spiral that even the courts decided she was unfit to mother her own children. My prayers were answered during my junior year in high school when the guy I thought would love me forever dropped me like a bad habit. In the blink of an eye, he told me we were over and by the end of the school day he walked past my locker holding hands with his new lover.

The pain was so excruciating, I couldn't breathe. The experience was so debilitating, my eyes were open but I couldn't see. What I was feeling was so darn loud, I couldn't hear myself think. I had emotionally been kicked in the stomach and just as my knees snapped in preparation to buckle, I somehow managed to think of my mother. To my own surprise, I suddenly smiled. In that second, I felt closer to my mother than I ever had during the eleven years that I lived with her. A deep sense of gratitude shivered up my spine, causing me to stiffen. I smiled even bigger as I thought of my mother again. Proudly inflating my chest, I then lifted my head upward and whispered, "Thank you, God. Finally, I get it." Finally, I understood my mother's pain and debilitation.

Finally and for the first time, my mother felt so very fragile and human to me. During the first week of my heartbreak, I suddenly understood what it was like to cry and long for someone who didn't want to be with me anymore. By the second week of my heartbreak, from firsthand experience, I understood why stalkers stalk, why drinkers dial drunk, why obsession itself becomes a compulsion and why letters written at night should never be sent until they're re-read the next morning.

Once I gained this understanding, I was filled with wonder. Considering the pain I felt after one relationship gone awry, I wondered how my mother actually lived through eight heartbreaks without going clinically insane. And, although for my mother's sake I wished her life had been different, I realized that she had to travel the road she did in order for me to create the path that I am creating. She was more than my front row teacher; my lovesick mother was also my leader.

By age seventeen I decided I wanted to learn all I could about being human and about that which informs our thinking, our actions, our reactions and our behavior. It is because of this desire that in 1982 I began taking transformational courses and studying Psychobiology at The City University of New York. I became intrigued by the power of the mind and the latent manifestations our thoughts have on our bodies. I always suspected there was a mind/body correlation because after my mother's heartbreaks, she often fell physically ill. I then began to wonder why heartbreak had not yet been classified as a clinical illness. After all, scientists and researchers are now calling the desire for companionship "necessary" and "essential" for optimal health.

Does this not assert that poor health could be attributed to the absence of companionship? In addition, clinical studies have shown a direct correlation between loneliness and heart disease. Does this not imply that a heart that's not at ease (due to loneliness) could very well be classified as a form of dis-ease? And, if this is even remotely possible, shouldn't someone be looking for a cure? It would be many years, several career detours and at least two more personal heartbreaks before I would find answers to that which I deeply began to question during my late teens. However, what I knew early on and beyond a shadow of a doubt was that like most diseases:

Heartbreak does not discriminate

Because we invest so much of our mental, spiritual and physical energy merging our lives with a loved one, I also began to realize how absurd it was for any of us to think we could get over our exes and sever ties in a matter of mere days, weeks or even months without proper support.

For the past six years, as a Transformational Coach I have had the opportunity to support hundreds of clients through the completion of their romantic relationships, restoring their hearts and enabling them to resume their normal lives with little or no suffering.

The process of getting over your ex is exactly that and such a process requires actions beyond crying, gossiping, stalking, ignoring or avoiding. Such a process demands that you let go of your immobilizing monologues and that you move into transforming dialogues and inquiries that are life altering experiences. In addition to fulfilling the aforementioned process, the 9 Keys in this book will enable you to transform your relationship to pain, labels and your circumstances. In order to better understand how you navigate the tumultuous sea of love, these 9 Keys will assist you in finding the sea vessel that best represents you.

Once you understand how you were designed, you will also understand the importance of choosing other ships that your ship can inherently relate to and therefore comfortably be in a relation-ship with. Metaphorically speaking, if you're a slow but steady Rowboat personality, the way you navigate the sea in the midst of a storm will vastly differ from that of a thrill-seeking Speedboat personality.

As a result of this difference, it's inevitable that someone's going overboard. Finally, in addition to identifying and learning about the kind of boat you float on the sea of love, you will also learn of the secret treasures you exchanged with your ex while journeying as one. The surprise is that these very treasures are truly the treasures you've been diving for and nearly willing to die for your entire life.

The 9 Keys you are about to work with are the exact Keys that I have used to heal my mother, myself, several family members and hundreds of my clients. The great news is that my mother became ex-free in 2002 and has been with the same wonderful man for five years. I am continuously moved to tears by my mother's newfound stability and security that she shares with her romantic partner.

A romantic relationship gone awry is enough to lock even the softest of hearts. However, by working the 9 Keys offered in this book, the toughest of hearts will unlock. What I mean by "working" each Key is that you actually exert the energy necessary to pull the information offered in each Key not only to you but also through you until the Key and your life issues meet as one.

Really work the Key, feel the impact the Key has on your life, understand how the Key pertains to your life. It's like inserting a key into a lock and turning it, wiggling it, working with it until you hear, or in this case you feel, that reassuring click. If you work the Keys the way the Keys are designed to be worked, I assure you, you are merely pages away from authentically getting over your ex. And as with most things in life, the more honest you can be with yourself while working each Key, the more powerful your results will be.

Before you take your first step towards being ex-free, I'd like to remind you that your mind can be a very dangerous neighborhood - do not go in there alone. My suggestion is that you find someone to work the Keys of this book with you. Assistance is available at the website TroyByer.com if you aren't able to partner with someone in your personal life. The website offers sponsorship, sharing and other forms of support for those of you who are committed to being unstoppable and powerfully clicking with these 9 Keys.

Regardless of who you work the Keys with, I ask that you be gentle with yourself every step of the way. For the sake of your clarity, record your thoughts and insights in the journal entry space available at the end of each Key. And please, don't believe every thought you think. Hold onto the good thoughts and let the not-so-good thoughts drift away like the ocean carries a wave.

Make Pain Your New Best Friend

"Your pain is the breaking of the shell that encloses your understanding."

-- Kahlil Gibran

The actual breaking of any body part is painful, especially the heart. However, in the case of heartbreak, the lock that keeps us trapped is we forget that pain is not the problem. Pain is merely a sensation that is present to remind us there is a problem. Of course, no one wants to be reminded of his or her problems. This is exactly why most people usually do anything but deal with the problem in order to get rid of their pain. Problems are meant to be solved. Solving problems are a large part of our learning and growth process. Unfortunately, learning certain lessons in life can be a painful experience, but again, the pain isn't the problem. Learning the lesson is the problem. In other words, when you learn the lesson, you solve the problem and you're then free to move forward. Why am I asking you to make pain your new best friend?

17

Because your pain will not only remind you that you have a problem that needs to be solved, it will also act as a gauge of your progress. Your pain is there for you and only you. Your pain can't be bought, traded or sold. Your pain's purpose is to make you aware of a problem that is demanding your immediate attention and your growth. As a matter of fact, we humans do one of two things when life beckons us to grow. We either wilt and dissolve in the face of the problem or we expand and grow as we boldly resolve the problem. The unfortunate thing about wilting is, the smaller you get, the bigger the problem gets. And by the way, the problem never really goes away. The seemingly unfortunate thing about growing is that most people and things don't grow in the space of comfort; growth is usually accompanied by pain. Hence the term "growing pains."

Let me just say, I've yet to meet anyone who had a life-altering experience while lounging on their couch downing a pint of ice cream. It just doesn't happen that way. A perfect metaphor for the growth-pain process is the journey of a seed. Seeds are buried in deep, damp, dark places and then forced to grow as they push upward in search of air, light and space. Once the seed pushes through the dark, painful and uncomfortable space, what immediately follows is its natural beauty. Relationships are to humans what soil is to seeds. Relationships are deep fields fertilized with the substances and composition necessary to activate our growth. If you are hurting, if you are in pain, all that means is that your relationship has activated your spirit's desire to grow. Without a doubt, if you are really ready to get over your ex, it's going to take some growing on your part. The good news is that although the pain from growing is inevitable, suffering is always optional. If you don't want to suffer from the pain then it's imperative that you make your pain your best friend. The thought of befriending your pain is probably as inviting as sticking a needle beneath your fingernail. However, you know you would never want to stick a needle beneath your fingernail because pain, your friend, has taught you that such an action would hurt.

Until now, you've probably viewed pain as something that's there to hurt you instead of viewing it as something that's there to actually help you. The fact is, like any good friend would, pain shows up suddenly to let you know you are in danger. If the notion of pain being equivalent to a friend is still tough to grasp, imagine that a friend woke you up at three o'clock in the morning, warning you of an impending danger. Without question, you would listen to your friend because you would trust your friend was there to help you. Let's take this same scenario and replace the word "friend" with "pain." It would then read like this: Imagine that a pain woke you up at three o'clock in the morning, warning you of an impending danger. Without question, you would listen to your pain, knowing that your pain was there to help you. Like a friend, your pain's concern is for you. Like a friend, your pain is trying to tell you something and like a best friend, your pain is not going to shut up until you finally stop and listen.

So, what is your pain trying to tell you about your relationship with your ex? Your pain is trying to tell you that if you are still feeling IT, then you are still connected to IT. In other words, if you are still feeling the pain caused by your relationship with your ex, it's because you are still connected to the relationship with your ex. The stronger the pain, the stronger your connection to your ex remains. If you really think about it, the logic is inescapable because the pain you are currently feeling is a bi-product of the relationship you shared with your ex. Again, as long as the pain caused by the relationship is present, you are still connected to that relationship.

You may not physically be connected to the relationship with your ex. However, experiencing the pain keeps you emotionally connected to the relationship. Remember, the pain is there to remind you that there is still a problem to solve. The problem reminds you that there is still a lesson to learn. This is all for the sake of your personal growth. Also remember, nothing grows in the space of comfort. The great news is that if you let your pain be your guide, you will learn the lesson, and as a result you will permanently remove the experiences connected to the lessons. Not only will you finally be ex-free but if you're a conscious life student you will never have to repeat those experiences again. I can't tell you how many times I've found myself dating the same person. The only differences were the faces and the names. The other thing they all had in common is that they all cheated on me - all of them. In spite of my mother's heartbreaks, I still managed to fall prey to being heartbroken three times by three different men, all sharing similar traits. My first heartbreak was during my teens. My second heartbreak was in my early twenties. My third and final heartbreak was in my early thirties.

These relationships all began the same way, which is that they relentlessly pursued me. After they got me, I found myself working overtime to keep them, often compromising my principles. The relationships then ended because I found out they had cheated on me. Yes, these cookie-cutter relationships continued until I became a conscious life student, and eventually created and worked the Keys offered in this book. In doing so, I learned the lessons I needed to learn in order to grow and eliminate those repetitive experiences. This was the beginning of my being truly ex-free. After three painful relationships, I finally learned that my romantic partners cheated on me because I cheated on myself just to be with them. For example, my ex-fiancé came from a very close family and they had two very big problems with me. The first problem was that I'm half black. The second problem was, I was an actress. They were certain they didn't want any black people or Hollywood types in their family, no exceptions. Obviously, I couldn't change my skin color so what did I do? I quit acting. Just like that. I literally cheated myself out of a career I had been dreaming of since I was a little girl just so my ex-fiancé's family would accept me. The truth is that we teach people how to treat us by the way we treat ourselves. I cheated on myself and then my ex-fiancé cheated on me. It's as simple as that.

As you now embark upon your freedom journey, I strongly encourage you get to know your pain like you would a friend. The exercise for this Key is intended to support you with the creation of this acquaintance. I suggest you take a moment to safely but honestly get re-connected to your pain before doing the exercise. The point of this exercise is to strengthen your ability to recognize your pain like you would a friend in a crowd. After all, if you are going to use your pain as a scale to measure your progress, shouldn't you know exactly what your scale looks like? In addition, by knowing what your pain looks like when it's fully present, you'll also have a better idea of what it will look like as it rapidly begins to disappear.

Exercise: HOW DOES YOUR PAIN LOOK?

If Your Pain Had A Color What Color Would Your Pain Be?

(circle at least one and no more than two)

GREY	RED	TURQUOISE
ORANGE	BLACK	BROWN
BLUE	YELLOW	GREEN

OTHER _____

Colors possess both negative and positive energies. When your pain is being experienced as a color, the negative pole of that color is most likely impacting your mood. Below is a list of suggested thoughts that will instantly give you access to the positive pole of your color. So, whenever your pain is present, instead of allowing the negative pole of your pain color to dominate your thoughts, simply and immediately follow the remedies inherent to your pain color.

Grey: *Find a safe space and be still and know that it's okay to be wherever you are. Allow your opinions to go where they will but do not relate to your opinions as the only truth.*

Black: *Connect with your breath and as you exhale, release the pain. As you inhale, breathe in the light. Continue to breathe out the darkness   and breathe in the light.*

Red: *Honor who you are for you. Let go of any thoughts of who you might or might not be for others. Focus only on you and allow your inherent love of love to calm and soothe you.*

Brown: *Find a way to get grounded immediately and anchor yourself in your truth, knowing that your roots are connected to the essence of all that is good.*

Blue: *Find your truth. Honor your truth. Empower your truth. Be open to other truth.*

Green: *Open your heart to receiving the field of love and abundance that is always around you.*

Turquoise: *Acceptance of yourself and others is the key to your peace.*

Orange: *Know that as a creator, from nothingness you can create anything and everything.*

Yellow: *Allow the light to reveal the truth in you and outside of you and from there, choose the path that clearly comforts you.*

Below Please Circle The Part Of Your Body In Which You Experience Pain Most

ARMS	LEGS	NECK
SHOULDERS	CHEST	HEAD
STOMACH	BACK	THROAT
HANDS	KNEES	FEET

What Your Body Pain Location Signifies:

Arms: *Don't want to carry the load*

Head: *Self-criticism*

Throat: *Suppressed expressions*

Legs: *Fear of moving forward*

Chest: *Unable to deal with pressure*

Hands: *Difficulty letting go*

Neck: *Inability to be flexible*

Stomach: *Unable to digest a situation*

Knees: *Rigid and constrained by pride & ego*

Shoulders: *Heavily burdened & incapable of coping*

Back: *Lack of support offered to you*

Feet: *Confused, lacking in understanding*

When My Pain Is Present, My Pain Makes Me Feel Like:
(check at least one and no more than two)

_____ *I'm trapped in a straight jacket.*

_____ *I'm wearing a vest made of lead that's pulling me to my knees.*

_____ *I'm buried in six feet of dirt and I can't breathe.*

_____ *I'm swimming in a jar of petroleum jelly and I can't see.*

Other _____

My Pain Makes Me Feel As If All I Want To Do Is:

Scream	Die	Hurt Someone Else
Fight	Run Away	Disappear
Cry	Hurt Myself	

Other _____

Now I'd like you to write a brief summary about your pain which will be as simple as filling in the following blanks.

Your Summary About Your Pain:

The color of my pain is _____

The part of my body in which I feel my pain the most is my _____

MAKE PAIN YOUR NEW BEST FRIEND

When my pain is present, my pain makes me feel like ——————————————————————

——————————————————————

My pain makes me feels as if all I want to do is

——————————————————————

——————————————————————

Congratulations! Now that you know the characteristics of your pain, not only will you recognize the arrival of your pain from a distance, but when it arrives you can actually start to have fun with it. The next time you notice yourself in pain, stop everything you're doing and just be with your pain. Acknowledge your pain's presence. Look at the color you attached to it. Is that the color that best represents your pain? If not, change it. If it is, be with it. Allow your attention to flow to the part of your body that you feel your pain the most. Is this an accurate location? If not, change it. If so, be with it. Whatever you choose to do upon the arrival of your pain, the most important thing is that you don't make your pain wrong for being there. In other words, don't resist it.

Simply acknowledge its presence, embrace it and accept it if you can. Remember that pain is inevitable. However, if you diligently work and click with this first Key by making pain your new best friend, your suffering will always be optional.

My Thoughts & Insights

Your Crutch Is Just A Crutch

The worst thing you can try to do is cling to something that is gone, or to recreate it.

-- Napolitano

Life without our ex can be challenging in the early stages because like most committed couples, we were extensions of one another. When that the extension is gone, there's inevitably an enormous void, an empty space that's comparable to a missing limb. As a result of this most of us become "emotional amputees" and we reach for emotional crutches to fill the void. Emotional crutches are individualized transitional objects that provide instant gratification in other-wise empty, stressful or emotionally intense circumstances. Crutches are intended to help people get back onto their feet and move forward in life. Keep in mind that there are positive crutches such as music, spirituality and exercising. There are also negative crutches such as alcohol, drugs and gambling. However, even positive crutches can have a negative effect if they are continuously used to avoid or ignore an emotional injury.

Before we move on, it's important that you know Key 2 is not about kicking away your crutch. Truthfully, if asking you to kick away your crutch were enough to have you do it - if it were really that easy to kick - then it wouldn't really be a crutch. You see, it's not easy to just kick away something that you depend on, lean on, find solace and safety in just because someone asks you to. So unless you're ready, don't worry about kicking away your crutch today, tomorrow or even next year. The value of working and clicking with Key 2 is that you recognize yourself as the owner and creator of your crutch before your crutch takes ownership and makes a hostage out of you.

When it comes to crutches, there is a very fine line between owning a crutch and being owned by a crutch. If you are using a crutch to cope, only you know if you are using it or misusing it. The fact is, there are stressful times in life when things get a little wacky and if you need a little support to restore your balance then a good crutch can be a great thing. Just know, there is a distinct difference between reaching for a crutch for support and depending on a crutch for survival. If you are using an emotional crutch, your life literally depends on you knowing and being responsible for this difference.

After my heartbreaks, short of ripping my heart out of my chest, I didn't know how to stop the pain. I just didn't know what to do. In the past, when faced with a challenging situation, I turned to my romantic partner for advice and solace. Without my romantic partner, I was completely lost. In fact, there was one time, after my second heartbreak, that I actually called my ex and asked him to help me get over him. He answered my request by passing the phone to his new girlfriend and she told me to stop calling her man. Ouch. Metaphorically speaking, her words chopped my legs off at the knees. I was devastated. I wanted the world to stop so I could get off or at least crawl beneath it and die. I didn't know what it was going to take for me to get back on my feet but I knew I had to find something and I had to find it fast.

A gay friend of mine introduced me to my very first crutch. He told me that the best way to get over one lover was to crawl beneath another. I decided he was more of an expert on men than me so I took his advice. Hmm. Let's just say, the words torture and shame best describe my experience of being with one lover in an effort to get over another. Because I didn't want to be like my mother, promiscuous behavior was never the crutch for me. Still, I was relieved to know that crutches existed. I was also certain I would find the crutch for me and if not, I was determined to create it for sure. The next set of crutches I reached for were big, big hits. I found solace in mindless shopping sprees during the day, smoking cigarettes and drinking large quantities of wine at night. Like most crutches, they initially felt like lifesavers. I really felt as if I were back on my feet and moving forward with my life. I soon forgot about my ex and all I wanted were my crutches. I fell in love with smoking. I fell in love with shopping. I fell in love with drinking. That was my life and, at that time, I swore my life was great.

One morning, after a really long night of smoking, boozing and trying on clothes that I brought home and suddenly hated -- something happened. I woke up with a raging hangover and, as I was focusing on the pain of my throbbing head, I accidentally took a good look at my life. It dawned on me that I hadn't made any real progress with my crutches at all. As a matter of fact, I realized that the only thing my crutches had really supported me with were my secret suspicions of alcoholism, one continuous sore throat and maxed out credit cards. I was stunned. I couldn't understand how my crutches turned out to be big kickstands with invisible anchors. Even after realizing my crutches were actually holding me down, I wasn't ready to let them go. I was certain that if I let go of my crutches, the bottom would literally drop out of the ground. I now know, at that time, I wasn't willing to kick my crutches because I wasn't ready to be responsible for my life. I wanted to remain disabled for as long as I possibly could because, in a strange way, I felt safe and that felt really good. Initially, we all have different reasons for reaching for our crutches and these reasons, at best, only approximate the truth. At face value, the reason I reached for my crutches was that I literally, physically couldn't get out of bed without them. Still, there was a truth that I was avoiding.

When I was finally able to admit it, I realized if I stayed in bed, I wouldn't be able to fail at anything because I wouldn't be attempting to do anything. In other words, the real reason I needed my crutches wasn't because I was disabled. I needed my crutches because my secret truth was that I was incapable of succeeding in life. I am not saying this was the truth. I am saying, this was my secret truth. I really believed I was incapable of making my relationships work. I really believed that I was incapable of protecting myself from getting hurt. And yet, I was also incapable of creating an equal or better life for myself without my ex hence my "failure-proof" life that consisted of sleeping, smoking, shopping and drinking.

After my third breakup ended in divorce, I didn't have the luxury of living the "failure-proof" life that I had when my last two exes and I had split up. This time around, I had a huge responsibility. I had an eight-month-old son to care for. It took me less than a week to realize that I could not afford to smoke around the clock, drink myself to sleep at night and then shop in the malls all day with a child depending on me. During that first week, I tried to pretend I needed my crutches in order to, really, be there for my child but for the love of my son, I soon had to acknowledge that my emotional crutches were never really going to replace my missing limbs. I finally had to admit, after using these crutches to heal from two previous relationships, that the most momentum I ever got with my crutches were baby steps and even those steps were taken with a noticeable limp.

So, the day came when it was time for me to call my crutch a crutch. It was time for me to admit that crutches were really only good for two things: numbing my pain and reminding me that I was broken. The unfortunate thing about numbing pain, which we learned in Key 1, is that without the presence of pain, it's almost impossible to gauge our healing process. And of course, the crutches want me to continuously remember that I'm broken because the instant I'm healed, my crutches are history. Fortunately, I was able to call my crutch a crutch before falling into the trap of mistaking my crutches for feet and therefore believing that I couldn't move without them. This is exactly when addiction sets in.

Almost all addictions originate as emotional crutches. And almost all emotional crutches attempt to compensate for emotional injuries. One of the best ways to avoid addiction is to make sure you can always honestly recognize and call your crutch a crutch and NEVER confuse it with your emotional injury. If you ever find yourself on the verge of being addicted to your crutch, I strongly suggest that you seek two forms of treatment. One form of treatment must be focused on your relationship to the crutch that you are possibly addicted to. The second form of treatment must be focused on healing the emotional injury that had you reach for your crutch in the first place. Again, please do not collapse the two and get one form of treatment for both. This is crucial. If you're on the verge of addiction, it's the collapsing of your crutch and your emotional injury that most likely got you where you are today. You must un-collapse them and you must do it separately and right away.

The last thing that I'd like you to know about your crutch is that a crutch can reveal things about you that you may not consciously be able to see. For example, whenever I find myself craving a cigarette, I instantly know that somewhere in the recent past, I was emotionally injured. I also instantly know that I am craving my crutch because I didn't deal with my emotional injury in a manner that left me fully restored and satisfied. In that moment, I can either light a cigarette and hang out with my crutch for a while or I can figure out what my emotional injury is and deal with it in a powerful manner. The bottom line is, when you can honestly call your crutch a crutch and understand the purpose of your crutch, your crutch can better enable you to understand yourself.

Exercise: TO THY OWN CRUTCH BE TRUE

When You're Upset And You Want To Shift Your Mood, What Activity Quickly Does the Trick For You? *(e.g. eating, sleeping, exercising, gambling, etc...)*

_____

Assuming Your Answer Above Is Your *Emotional Crutch*, What Reasons Do You Have For Reaching For Your Crutch When You Do?

I reach for my emotional crutch when

_____

While using my emotional crutch my focus is on

_____

My emotional crutch also enables me to ignore

_____

Now Without Giving It Too Much Thought, Make A Quick List Of 10 Additional Reasons That You Reach For Your Emotional Crutch.

(please write quickly and do not stop until you have listed 10 reasons)

I reach for my emotional crutch because without it I feel:

1. _____

2. _____

3. _____

4. _____

5. _____

6. _____

7. _____

8. _____

9. _____

10. _____

Now That You Know What Your Emotional Crutch Is And You Know 10 Reasons Why You Reach For It, Look To See If You Can Identify Your Secret Truth About Your Crutch.

My Example: My secret truth wasn't that I was disabled. My secret truth was that I didn't feel capable of succeeding on my own.

EX-FREE

1. On your reasons list, if you had a reason that was the most difficult to admit or write, chances are that reason is also your secret truth.

-OR-

2. On your reasons list, if you had repetitive words, chances are that repetitive word holds the clue to your secret truth.

-OR-

3. While making your reasons list, if at any point you flat-out wanted to quit making the list, chances are your secret truth is whatever you wrote immediately before or after your thoughts of quitting.

If you have found your *secret* truth regarding your emotional crutch, good for you. If you haven't, not to worry, as you move forward your secret truth will reveal itself at some point during the next 7 Keys.

My Thoughts & Insights

You Are Not Your Circumstances

Death is not the biggest fear we have; our biggest fear is taking the risk to be alive -- the risk to be alive and express what we really are.

-- Don Miguel Ruiz

If I were to ask you, "How're you doing today?" and you were to honestly answer me, you would most likely allow your circumstances to inspire your answer to my question. Why? Because most people define themselves by their life circumstances. To make matters worse, most people also believe that their circumstances are beyond their control. So, how they're doing in life is basically out of their control. The important thing to know is that whether you believe your circumstances are beyond your control doesn't matter right now. What matters is that you profoundly understand that you are not your circumstances. There's you. There's your circumstances. Circumstances change every day for various reasons. You are always uniquely you.

If you lived in London and it was raining when I called you from sunny Los Angeles and I asked how you were doing today you wouldn't say, "Oh, today I'm raining," would you? Of course not because you are not rain, you are you. Sure, there's a current circumstance called rain in your life that is the result of certain weather conditions. You might even tell me about the rain you are currently experiencing but you would never, ever identify yourself as the rain. Why? Because rain is just a circumstance in your life at that moment and again, you are not your circumstances. There will always be circumstances that are the result of certain conditions and then there will always be you. Your heartbreak is a circumstance of a condition that you happen to be experiencing. You are no more your heartbreak than you are your poverty or your wealth, your flu, your happiness, sadness or anger. Again, these are all temporary circumstances that are caused by certain conditions.

Once you stop identifying yourself as your circumstances, you will also stop treating yourself as a circumstance. Here's another example: if you had a headache, would you suddenly identify yourself as a headache and therefore treat yourself like a headache? The answer is obvious, isn't it? No matter what condition you have, you are still you. Your headache is a circumstance that you happen to be experiencing. The same holds true for heartache. You are no more your heartache than you would be your headache. It's very important to fully ingrain this fact in your DNA because your perception of yourself during this healing process is crucial. What you think of you is the very thing that's going to pull you through and eventually assist you in getting over your ex. So, the next time someone asks you how you're doing, your response could sound like this, "My circumstances are challenging but I'm doing well." That will be the truth if you are working the Keys in this book and focusing on your healing.

Now that you know that you are not your circumstances, the next logical question might be, who are you? I will answer this question with another question which is, who are you committed to being? The thing about commitments is that they're not designed to change at the drop of a dime. A commitment is that to which you are willing to devote, dedicate, or oblige yourself - no matter what. People make commitments to marriages, to jobs, to their children. Rarely do we consciously make commitments to ourselves. Who would you like to be for yourself, regardless and independent of your circumstances? Life is always going to show up with challenging circumstances. The big question is, who are you going to be in the face of life's circumstances? The good news is you actually get to make this choice. The not-so-good news is that if you don't make the choice, your circumstances will choose for you.

A female client of mine once dated a divorced father who was literally a rocket scientist. With degrees from very prestigious universities, this guy was as gorgeous in person as he was on paper. The challenge turned out to be that as an engineer for a biomedical company, his job was to foresee potential problems for such pharmaceutical giants as *Pfizer* and *Eli Lilly*. This in itself was a problem because his livelihood actually depended on his ability to look for and find things that could go wrong.

Unfortunately, his endless search for problems didn't stop at work. He was committed to being a problem finder and solver in all areas of his life including their relationship. If he couldn't find a problem, he diligently created problems because his sense of worth depended on the presence of problems. What he wasn't willing to understand was that, his problem-finding job was merely a circumstance and he didn't have to be his circumstance. Eventually, my client's relationship with this genius of a man became too big of a problem for her to solve. He continued to be burdened by the weight of his circumstances and as a result, their relationship came to an end. Again, if you don't consciously choose who you are going to be in the world, then by default, your circumstances will choose for you. The exercises on the next page were designed to support you with the privilege of choosing who you are committed to being in your life – no matter what the circumstances are.

Exercise: YOU CHOOSE YOU

In The Face Of ALL Circumstances, Who Are You Committed To Being?

Below, please list 5 of the most challenging circumstances in your life right now.

1. _____

2. _____

3. _____

4. _____

5. _____

Okay, now let's pretend it's exactly one year later and as you take this book out to look at your list, you realize each and every one of the challenging circumstances has either been removed from your life or resolved. Please give yourself a moment to really see this as your new reality. All of your items listed above are now nothing more than vague experiences of your past. Take a moment. See it. Feel it.

Now, quickly write down the two words that best describe how you would be being if this were true. Not what you would be doing, but how you would be being? We want to keep this in the domain of "being" because we are human beings NOT human doings.

Again, It's One Year Later And All Of The Challenging Circumstances You Listed Are Gone. How Would You Be Being?

1. _____

_____

2. _____

_____

I want you to really look at the two words that you wrote down. In all of the English vocabulary, there are hundreds of thousands of words that you could have chosen, and yet you chose those two. The reason you chose those two words is that at the core of your being, at the level of spirit, those two words best capture the person you are deeply committed to being for yourself and - surprisingly - for others.

The two words I chose while working this Key were Light and Love. At the time I chose these words, my conscious mind did not know that I was committed to shedding light and love into my life and the lives of others but, like you, my spirit knew my purpose, my real truth. So, as you continue working the Keys in this book and as you take on life, remember who you really are. And as often as you can, say those two words out loud. Those two words came to you because they are the words that are waiting to be expressed as you, by you. Own those words. Live those words. Be who you are committed to being. You choose you.

My Thoughts & Insights

Know The Boat You Float

Knowing yourself is the beginning of all wisdom.
-- Aristotle

Getting over your ex really is as simple as letting go of your ex and moving on with your life. This letting go may include releasing your ex emotionally, spiritually, psychologically and - for some - even physically. If the solution is so obvious, so cut and dry, shouldn't letting go be as easy? The answer is, yes and it is very easy to let go once you know exactly what you've been holding on to. The problem is, most people can't clearly see that which they are holding on to; therefore, they don't know what to let go of. This is the paradox; this is the trap that keeps people stuck.

Initially, exploring *what* you are holding on to may seem counter-productive in your pursuit to get over your ex because the logical question is seemingly *how* to get over your ex. However, I can assure you that asking *what* will place you on an entirely different road than asking *how*. The *what* road is paved with lessons you will need to learn in order to free yourself from your experience. In this case, the experience is your relationship with your ex.

Before we go any further, let's look at the different implications of these two words. *How* gives instructions regarding what you do, what you did or what you're doing. *What* gives you reasons that lead to insights and understanding about *what* you did or didn't do. Asking *what* instead of *how* will also boldly lead you into spaces you don't recognize because you have never been there before. This new territory will eventually place you at the source of why you chose your ex.

The word "source" is defined as the place where something begins. If you are able to get to the very seed that gave life to your relationship with your ex in the beginning, you will be able to wrap your mind around the roots of the relationship and remove them all at once, once and for all. Exploring the *what* will provide you with enormous clarity. In addition to seeing *what* you're holding on to, you will also better understand *what* you got into. After all, if you are ready to get out of a situation, you need to clearly see and understand *what* situation you're in. This is the power of *what*.

So, let's look at *what* you got into with your ex. You got into a relationship. If we break down the word relationship, we get the marriage of two words, "relation" and "ship." The word "relation" is defined as a natural association between two or more things. The word "ship" is defined as a vessel of considerable size for deep-water navigation. Reunite those two words and you have a relationship. What do you do with a relationship? Well, ships certainly aren't designed to remain in the harbor. They're designed to sail the seas. Assuming we recognize love as a journey, let's take it a step further and assert the following: relationships are related ships that are sailing across the sea of love. So, what you got yourself into was a relationship designed to sail across the sea of love.

It's common knowledge that the sea can be as tumultuous as it is smooth. Surely, the journey is worth taking, but in spite of their design, most ships would rather remain in the harbor than take a chance on traveling across the big blue sea alone. You know this. I know this. We all know this, which is why, again, we first seek out that seemingly perfect romantic partner-ship before leaving the harbor. What type of ship do you suppose you are on the sea of love? What about your ex?

In life you truly get what you inspect - not what you expect but what you inspect. You hear of people's expectations being unfulfilled all the time. I've yet to hear of anyone having unfulfilled inspections. This is because you really do get exactly what you inspect.

WHICH SEA VESSEL BEST REPRESENTS YOU AND YOUR EX?

A Dinghy is a small lifeboat designed to rescue and save the lives of those who have been forced to

DINGHY

jump ship. Dinghy personalities commit their lives to rescuing others. This is the very fabric of their design. Once a Dinghy rescues you, the chances of you drowning are slim to none. If by chance you do drown, rest assured, it's because they drowned first. Dinghy personalities are as loyal as the day is long. Like the inflatable boats they represent, Dinghy personalities are sensitive and will easily deflate if punctured. They have also been known to deteriorate when placed in direct sunlight. Dinghy personalities don't want to be the center of attention. They only want to rescue and they'll take your deepest appreciation over public recognition any day. Although you will initially be grateful for the safety a Dinghy personality provides, your gratitude will soon shift to frustration if you're a personality who seeks adventure. You may begin to wonder how the one that saved your life could now be so stagnant and still. The upside of Dinghy personalities is that - to the best of their ability - they will keep you comfortable and safe. The downside is, once you're in the same boat, you'll simply drift and float, hoping that one day, something or someone will come along and excite you both.

FERRY

Ferries are designed to transport large groups of people and vehicles over expansive bodies of water. Ferry personalities are just that, transporters. Their commitment in life is to support others on their journey, carrying others who can't carry themselves. Ferries are like bridges - their life path is straight and predictable; they move from point A to point B and then back again. Ferries are capable of supporting many people at once, which is why a Ferry's concern is usually for the entire group as opposed to the individual. This usually means that one-on-one intimate interactions with a Ferry are few and far between.

The upside to Ferry personalities is that you'll always know exactly where they're taking you and you'll never be alone en route. The downside of Ferry personalities is that at times you might feel extremely lonely, especially when you're together in a crowd.

ROWBOAT

Rowboat personalities are designed to push against the flow, the water. Rowboat personalities are head-strong, self- sufficient and confident. Rowboat personalities set their sights on where they want to go or what they want done and that's it; they won't stop until they get it - for better or for worse. They lock their oars into the oarlock and off they go. Rowboat personalities are always certain they are headed in the right direction. How certain are they? They're so certain they actually sit with their backs facing in the direction they are headed.

Because of their unwavering certainty, it's often difficult to contribute to Rowboat personalities, they've got it handled. Rowboat personalities are well aware it takes two equal forces to efficiently coordinate those oars and unless they trust your endurance, muscle strength and effectiveness, don't you dare reach for an oar. The upside to Rowboat personalities is that you can kick back and relax; you'll reach your destination in due time. The downside to a Rowboat personality is, unless this individual considers you to be an equal force, you'll always be a passenger as opposed to a fully capable romantic partner.

SAILBOAT

A Sailboat is a boat propelled partially or wholly by sail. Wind is a Sailboat's primary means of propulsion. As a result, a Sailboat personality is a "Chaser." These individuals are constantly looking for that next best thing, that next force of wind that promises to set them off on another lap of smooth sailing. Sailboat personalities are engineered to chase the wind. If they don't chase the wind, they're stuck without movement which goes against every fiber of their design.

The upside of Sailboat personalities is that it's an exhilarating adventure because you never really know where that next force of wind will take you. The downside to Sailboat personalities is that you never really know which way that next force of wind will take you...it may even be overboard. Especially if you are not the next gush of wind a Sailboat personality is choosing to chase.

SEAPLANE

The first seaplane called "Le Canard" which means "The Duck" was built in 1910 by a French engineer.

That's exactly what Seaplane personalities excel at, "ducking" in and out of situations. Today, Seaplanes are commonly used for fire-fighting duty. Their design allows them to get close enough to the fires to make a difference without getting burned. This is a good thing for Seaplane personalities because they literally can't take the heat. As long as it's comfortable for them, you can count on these individuals to really take care of you. Even when they leave, they'll be watching over you from afar. Why do they come and go like the wind? Because Seaplane personalities don't do well with confrontation. In fact, Seaplanes can only land in water with little or no waves. Like the sea vessels they are modeled after, Seaplane personalities cannot deal with intimate situations as it constrains their wings. They need space - lots of space. When a situation gets too tight, they're out of there.

In order for these personalities to function well, all has to be well. The downside of Seaplane personalities is their livelihood depends on smooth weather conditions. These people need the freedom to easily come and go as they please. The upside is that you'll always have someone looking over you; just don't expect them to always be beside you.

SPEEDBOAT

A Speedboat's anthem is, "There is better than here." Speedboat personalities are independent and adventurous. They don't always know where they're going or why; they just need to get there fast. Speedboat personalities are very easy to detect; they're sleek in appearance and simply have a need for speed.

The downside to Speedboat personalities are, the heavier their load, the slower they go, which means that as much as they'd really like to show you their world, you might have to catch another ride. Speedboat personalities don't mean to be rude: they simply will not be slowed down by anyone or anything. The upside of these power driven personalities is exactly that -- power. A Speedboat personality is powerful, respected and admired by most.

STEAMBOAT

A Steamboat is a ship that is propelled by a steam engine and cannot function without steam. As a result, Steamboat personalities are always fueling and heating up so they have the energy to erupt.

Their movement is dependent upon steam. Steam wakes them up in the morning. Steam puts them to sleep at night. Steam gives them motion. This steam isn't necessarily negative or positive; Steamboat personalities just know how to produce results. Steam is literally the gas that gets them going and it keeps them from getting stuck. As you may have gathered by now, Steamboat personalities are highly strung. They collect evidence to feed their boiler so they can get enough steam to heat them up, and then off they go.

The upside to Steamboat personalities is that you won't ever have to guess what's going on in their minds or if they have the capability to do all the big things they've planned. Unless they choose to be lazy, Steamboat personalities are individuals with admirable endurance and tolerance. The downside of Steamboat personalities is when they erupt you can't take it personally; it's just the way they're designed. However, unless you want to melt like butter on a hot iron skillet, I suggest you steer clear of their steam until they cool down.

SUBMARINE

The word Submarine was originally an adjective meaning "under the sea." Submarine personalities submerge their feelings and emotions. These individuals run deep and steady until it is time to attack. Submarine personalities are perhaps the most lethal of the personalities because their emotions remain concealed and undetected. When these silent individuals finally explode, they're sure to have a boat full of ammunition and they'll be positioned to fire at close range.

As a result, you'll find yourself vulnerable to an attack with no recourse or defense. You might blame yourself for not finding or recognizing the signs of impending disaster. Don't worry; there weren't any signs. Like their namesake, Submarine personalities are difficult to find and destroy. They're just deep individuals, they can't help it; it's just how they were designed. The upside to Submarine personalities is that they are constant, dependable and steady. The downside of Submarine personalities is that when they're over you, you'll literally know it; all you have to do is look up.

My Thoughts & Insights

5

Find The Treasure You Hunt

People do not attract that which they want, but that which they are.

-- James Allen

In the world of ships, I'm a Ferry. As a Ferry, I absolutely love gathering groups of people together for common causes. Because I am so committed to being a source of support for others, it's vital that I journey the sea of love with someone who will be a stable source of support for me and that includes someone who has the capability of floating beside me. Today I am deeply privileged to share a relationship with a Rowboat personality. Sure, he can be as stubborn as the day is long but he navigates the sea of love in a manner that is both non-intrusive and supportive of me.

My ex-husband was a Seaplane. He was great at putting out my fires but he never stuck around to roast marshmallows after my flames simmered into coals. In true Seaplane fashion, once he knew I was safe, he was off to save someone else in distress, always keeping one eye on me from his "detached" perspective above. The fact is, due to their designs, it's nearly impossible for a Ferry and a Seaplane to attach because the waves caused by the Ferry's constant motion make it very challenging for the Seaplane to land without conflict. Individually, the Ferry and the Seaplane are both caring and wonderful sea vessels. When navigating the often tumultuous sea of love, they're just not so wonderful together. Is it their fault that they're not so wonderful together? Of course not. They're both just being true to their design and at the end of the day, that's all they really can be. Asking my ex to stop his engine and stay put in one place is comparable to clipping his wings or asking him to die. Like ships, we humans are uniquely designed. In spite of our individual designs, we all tow beautiful chests filled with treasures that are revealed along our journey. There are some treasures we believe we have and there are some treasures we believe we don't have.

What usually has us wanting to be "related" to other "ships" are the treasures they possess and those we find alluring and attractive. These treasures are often things we either don't believe we possess in our own treasure chest or we'd simply would like to have more of them. These treasures can be anything from money to adventure, to humor. Whatever the treasure is, having it in our chest makes us feel better as a person. On the other hand, not having it in our chest often leaves us with the sense that something is missing.

FIND THE TREASURE YOU HUNT

Now that you have a better understanding of your ex's and your design, in a moment you will have an opportunity to go on a treasure hunt of your very own. Before you begin your treasure hunt, I must warn you that most treasures are hard to find. When it comes to matters of the heart, the treasures we decide we need others to fill our chest with are often hidden from our immediate view.

These treasures are hidden because when it comes to relationships, no one really wants to appear needy. We don't want to appear needy to our prospective romantic partner, our family or friends. We especially don't want to relate to ourselves as needy, so we pretend we're not needy at all. As a result we find ourselves unconsciously hunting for our lost treasure with the desperation of a drug addict seeking drugs. I believe the following story exemplifies this often unconscious strategy well.

There once was a young girl who lived in the deep South and had an excellent perception of herself. She was a star in her small town because she was the only person who sang every Sunday for the town's two rivaling churches. Although the churches often urged the young girl to commit to one church, the girl would simply respond by informing them, if God loved them both, she could love them both as well. The churches weren't happy with her response and yet, neither church wanted to lose her.

One Christmas both of the churches sent the young girl Christmas presents to her home. Both of the boxes were big and both of the boxes were nicely wrapped. When the young girl excitedly opened each of the gift boxes, they were both empty, filled with nothing. The young girl was devastated and she concluded that the two churches vindictively gave her empty boxes because she refused to choose one church over the other.

The young girl immediately decided that people she loved did not appreciate her. In that split second the young girl swore that she would never love anyone again until they proved to her that they loved and appreciated her. How would she measure their love and appreciation? By the quantity and quality of the gifts they gave her, of course. However, because she was attempting to compensate for a past failure, there could never ever be enough gifts because she could never go back and alter her experience from that moment in history, try as she may. That young girl was my mother.

As a result, my mother drove each of her husbands away with her demand that they prove their love and appreciation by showering her with gifts. Hands down, each of my mother's exes uttered the same last words on their way out of her life which were "No matter what I give you, it's never enough." The treasure my mother decided was missing from her chest was appreciation and she spent the majority of her life hunting that treasure down. After working and clicking with the Keys in this book, I realized that my mother was never addicted to love. My mother was addicted to replacing the treasure she believed she lost as a child. She was attempting to alter an unpleasant experience of herself and she used love for that very purpose.

As you look to see what treasure your ex offered you before you set out to sea together, focus on the ships you feel best represent you and your ex. For example, my ex-husband brought characteristics of a Seaplane. And as I mentioned the ship that best represents me is a Ferry. As I put those two vessels side by side, I can see that what a Seaplane really does for a Ferry is watches over it and put out fires, if need be. So, the treasure that the Seaplane provides a Ferry with is safety.

Please note, I'm not asking you to list the treasures your ex's ship "could've" offered or "should've" offered. The question is, given the design of your ex's ship and given the design of your ship, what was the treasure that your ship didn't have but wanted and your ex's ship was able to bring to the table of your relationship?

Exercise: THE TREASURE HUNT

Below Please List At Least 3 Treasures That Your Ex's Ship Brought To The Table: *(e.g., adventure, stability, drama, excitement, security, peace, joy, company, danger, safety, etc.)*

1. _____

2. _____

3. _____

Of The 3 Treasures You've Listed Above, Please Circle The One That Was The Most Valuable To You.

If you are finding it challenging to identify the treasure that your ex brought to the table, try looking from this angle: if the experience of love and relationships were to be banned from the planet forever, what is the one thing that you would miss most about being in love and/or being in a relationship?

Consider that the treasure you circled above or the thing you decided you would miss the most IS the very treasure you have been holding onto with regard to your ex. One of the main reasons we continue to hold on is because we believe that if we truly let go of our ex, we will also have to let go of the treasure our ex added to our treasure chests. By the time you work with the 9th Key, you will see this simply isn't true. Remember, most people can't let go of their relationships because they don't know exactly what it is they're holding onto. Now that you have an idea of what you are holding onto ask yourself the following question:

Why Is Holding Onto That Treasure So Important To Me?

I'm holding onto _____

_____

because _____

_____

The treasure that you are holding onto may be somewhat of a surprise to you at first. Then, like me, after a bit of thought, the treasure/treasures you hunt will make a world of sense to you. On a conscious level, we are rarely aware of our need for these treasures because it is so deeply woven into the fabric of our existence. It's like the way a fish isn't consciously present to water because water is simply a part of a fish's existence. On a sub-conscious level, the fish knows that it must always be in water and on the lookout for more water.

As humans, we are to our treasures what fish are to water. Subconsciously, we are always on the look out for it because we decided long ago that this is what we need in order to feel whole and complete.

My Thoughts & Insights

The Power of Agreement

Happiness is when what you think, what you say, and what you do are in harmony.

-- Gandhi

The treasures we have decided we need in our treasure chests are so vital to our existence that they actually choose our prospective romantic partners for us. Said another way, your treasure chest operates as if its floor is a huge magnet drawing nearer that which you need in order to experience yourself as whole and complete. Using our ears and eyes, our magnetic treasure chest knows exactly what to look and listen for on that first, second and third date with a prospective romantic partner. For example, my magnetic chest was listening and looking for the promise of safety. On my second date with my ex-husband, he told me in his very bold Seaplane fashion, "All you need to do is figure out how to take all the problems off your shoulders and put them on mine." In that moment, my magnetic treasure chest got the AGREEMENT it was looking and listening for and I was married to my Seaplane personality just six weeks later.

Agreements are the glue that bonds people, things and unions together. Broken agreements are the scissors that cut people, things and unions apart.

Anytime there is disharmony, somewhere there is also a broken agreement. Broken agreements are not only the main causes of lawsuits, broken agreements interrupt the fulfillment of future expectations. Expectations unfulfilled lead to upsets and emotional injuries.

There are three types of agreements: VERBAL, e.g. wedding vows; WRITTEN, e.g., pre-nuptial agreements; and SILENT. Silent agreements are usually based on assumptions and silent agreements are what I consider to be the most constructive or destructive agreements of them all.

It doesn't take much of an imagination to figure out what a destructive silent agreement is, however, here's a very interesting example of a constructive silent agreement. I once knew an elderly couple that would just argue all day long. Their bickering was so intense it literally made everyone around enormously uncomfortable. Yet, if anyone tried to intervene, the couple would join forces and retaliate against the intruder.

Most people couldn't understand how this couple managed to remain married for over fifty years. The success of their longevity is that they had both silently agreed to be rotten to each other and this agreement worked for them, for whatever reasons. Their being rotten with each other fulfilled their expectations and fulfilled their needs from one another. By the way, they didn't care if their children or anyone else agreed with the manner in which they treated each other because the agreement existed between the two of them and no one else.

Now, if one of these two suddenly decided they no longer wanted to be treated poorly by their romantic partner, without a doubt, their relationship would have ended. Why? Because the glue that kept them together - the agreement - would have been broken. Remember, agreements keep relationships together, broken agreements tear people apart, regardless of the nature of the agreement. What does this have to do with getting over your ex? Very simple. At some point during the start of your relationship, your ex agreed to fill your chest with treasures that you wanted and/or needed. When your relationship with your ex was over, agreements were inevitably broken. Broken agreements are often the catalyst for heartbreak.

The Journey of Heartbreak

Broken Agreement → Emotional Injury → Challenging Circumstances → Crutch

Which agreements did your ex first make and then break? Which agreements with your ex did you make and then break? Look and see if you can identify at least one agreement that your ex broke and one agreement that you broke to your ex, prior to your break-up. Remember, an agreement can be verbal, written or silent and agreements are contracts that are based on expectations of how things will be in the future. When agreements are terminated then so is the future.

As you travel back down memory lane in search of your agreements, the silent agreements may not initially jump out at you. However, stay in the inquiry. Look at the things you said to each other that led to the creation of verbal agreements. Look at the things you didn't say. Were these unspoken words silent agreements?

Exercise: *IDENTIFYING YOUR BROKEN AGREEMENTS*

My ex broke the agreement to _____

_____

_____

_____

I broke the agreement to _____

_____

_____

_____

Is There Anything Else? If So, Please List Any Other Agreements That You Or Your Ex Broke To One Another In The Space Below:

CHECK IN POINT

Before we go on, let's take a moment to do a little cross checking here. If you were able to identify your SECRET Truth while working Key 2, please answer the following:

My Secret Truth is

_____

_____

The Treasure/Treasures my ex filled my treasure with is/are

_____

_____

Now look and see if your Secret Truth is in anyway affected by the treasure/treasures your ex gave you and if so, please explain:

_____

_____

_____

If you still haven't found your *Secret* Truth, see if you can fill in the blanks:

The Treasure my ex filled my Treasure Chest with was_____

_____

_____

CHECK IN POINT

*Having this in my Treasure Chest took away my concerns of*_____

_____

_____

If you were able to fill in the blanks above, then whatever you wrote down after the word "of" is most likely your Secret Truth. If you're still not sure what your Secret Truth is at this point, I suggest you STOP and do not proceed until someone can support you with the next exercise. Not to worry; there's nothing wrong - just something wonderful to reveal. This would be an excellent time for you to grant someone the opportunity to contribute to you. If you are not able to find support in your personal life, please request support at:

TroyByer.com

If you have yet to distinguish your Secret Truth and have someone to support you with this next exercise, please take your time and begin filling in the following blanks:

If I were really able to Get Over My Ex, I would feel so happy and free because in the morning I would be able to

_____

_____

_____

During the day I would be able to

_____

_____

_____

And at night I could finally

_____

_____

_____

In order for you to get the maximum results from this book, it is imperative that you powerfully complete the above exercise before moving on. Please take as much time as you need to fully get present to what is available to you once you get over your ex.

See it in your mind's eye, touch it, know it, be it. I understand where you are and I also know you have what it takes to cross over this threshold. We all have the power to transform our lives. I applaud your courage and commend you on all it has taken for you to get this far. We're almost there. Whatever you do, don't stop now.

My Thoughts & Insights

Create The Labels That Work For You

When one door closes another opens. But often we look so long so regretfully upon the closed door that we fail to see the one that has opened for us.

- Helen Keller

I do believe there are instances when titles and labels aren't necessary. However, when it comes to healing matters of the heart, I believe titles and labels are a must. Having said this, I will also say that in order to manage our expectations, we should carefully choose the labels and titles we assign our exes. Why? Because if you see a four-legged animal that looks like a cow, not only will you label it cow, you will expect it to behave like a cow. If what you have referred to as a cow starts barking like a dog, not only will you be confused but depending on your investment in the cow being a cow, you will also be disappointed. The same holds true with the labels and titles we give our loved ones. If you label your romantic partner "your Princess" it's because that's how you've chosen to perceive her and as a as a result, Princess behavior is what you'll expect.

Perceptions Lead To Labels & Labels Lead To Expectations

Until you consciously re-label your ex your mind will expect your ex to behave consistently with the label your ex was originally assigned. This is why the process of re-labeling is crucial if you are committed to getting over your ex. The process of re-labeling your ex allows the brain to do a bit of re-filing if you will. When we are suffering over the loss of an ex, it's often because our brain's perception doesn't match our heart's expectations or experiences. The human brain requires a sense of comprehensive order or it will reject whatever information it receives. In other words, until the mind's perception is a match for the heart's experience, there is a glitch in the system; reality is warped and confusion and upset prevails.

Before you proceed, I must warn you, working and clicking with this Key may take more effort on your part if you have any hopes you and your ex will get back together. Why? Because your mind will insist on holding on to the original label you assigned your ex so your heart can experience the behavior consistent with this label when and if you and your ex re-unite. If this applies to you, I'd like you to know that re-labeling your ex won't alter the possibility of you re-uniting with your ex. Actually, re-labeling your ex will support you with the possibility of your re-union. Einstein said it best, "No problem can be solved from the same level of consciousness that created it." By re-labeling your ex you will shift your consciousness which will then alter your perceptions, your expectations and inevitably your experiences. Let's continue.

What did you label you ex? As a result of this label, how did your mind perceive your ex and what did your heart expect from your ex? If you're not sure what you might have labeled your ex, here are three hints. 1) The label you assigned to your ex will have a lot to do with what you have been holding on to since your break-up. 2) The label you assigned your ex will have even more to do with the agreements he/she made with you, or 3) The label you assigned your ex will have a lot to do with the treasures that he/she added to your treasure chest or the treasures you miss the most since your relationship with your ex ended.

Whatever the label was, chances are good that it was a label you assigned your ex in the past when you were in a committed relationship with each other. So, the question is, "What label can you assign your ex now?" This label should be one that first, works for you and second, empowers you both. For instance, I had one client who labeled his ex-wife his "nurturer." I had him immediately re-label her because, until he did, his mind would continue to perceive her as a nurturer and his heart would have expected her actions to be consistent with that of the old label. After several tries, he excitedly re-labeled her "cultivator" because he felt comfortable relating to her as someone who *taught* him how to nurture and be nurtured. The moment you choose a new, more suitable title to label your ex, there will be an instant shift in your perception of your ex and as a result, your expectations will instantly alter as well.

The moment I relabeled my ex as "my parenting partner" instead of "my protector," my thoughts immediately went from "I wonder who he'll spend the holidays with," to "Wouldn't it be nice to take our son to Gymboree together this weekend." It really was that simple. It was that simple because, metaphorically speaking, the title of the book had changed and therefore so did the story that would now unfold across the pages of the book.

At this point, you might be wondering what new label you could assign your ex or how you're going to ever find a new label that's suitable for your ex. Well, here are some ideas: Let's say that your ex was a spiritual anchor for you. The treasure that your ex added to your treasure chest left you feeling closer to God as you know God to be. A perfect new title for you to label your ex might be, "Spiritual Alarm Clock." If you can authentically re-title your ex as a

CREATE THE LABELS THAT WORK FOR YOU

"Spiritual Alarm Clock," what immediately follows is your perception of alarm clocks and we all know that alarm clocks are designed to wake people up. Once the alarm clock goes off, a person wakes up. Now, once you have changed the title from Spiritual Anchor to Spiritual Alarm Clock, your ex will start to occur differently for you; again your perception will be shifted. In turn, the title Spiritual Alarm Clock will naturally alter your expectations.

People enter our lives for reasons, seasons or a lifetime. As you consider new titles to re-label your ex, I invite you to accept that the time you and your ex spent together was for a reason - a great reason. Please don't invalidate your time spent together in the past because of your present situation. As you look for the new label that best suits your ex, I ask that you bring honor to your thoughts; honor for the happy times and the true reasons that you two were together.

Exercise: RE-LABELING

The OLD LABEL that I assigned to my ex was

_____

and as a result, I expected my ex to do and be the following for me:

1._____

2._____

3._____

The NEW LABEL that I have assigned to my ex is

_____

and as a result, I expect my ex to do and be the following for me:

1._____

2._____

3._____

My Thoughts & Insights

Empty The Bucket

The purpose of our lives is to give birth to the best which is within us.

--Marianne Williamson

In order to truly shift your perception and masterfully create another vision for yourself, it is important that you honestly acknowledge all that you have experienced and all that you hoped to experience. This will be your access to finally being complete. It's like a bucket filled with water. You cannot fill the bucket with fresh new water until you first acknowledge the old water that is in the bucket. After acknowledging the old water in the bucket, you will need to pour it out to make space for the new water you will someday be putting into that same bucket. Emptying the bucket, or in this case ˋ your heart and mind, is the next Key you will need to turn in order to get over your ex.

We will go about this by making an honest and thorough list of ten great things you would like to acknowledge your ex for. The next step will be for you to make a list of ten great things that you would like your ex to acknowledge you for.

These lists are not intended to be seen by your ex. These lists are for you and your healing only. If you set about creating these lists with the mindset that you may share them with your ex, you will inevitably find yourself censoring and editing your thoughts and that would alter the purpose of the process entirely. What will make this Key powerful and life-transforming for you will be your ability to tell the absolute truth without any outside considerations. Working this key by writing Acknowledgment lists is no easy task but they're necessary if you are really committed to being ex-free. On the next page I have provided the structure for you to complete your lists. Before you begin, I suggest you find a peaceful, safe place for you to sit and open your heart as you empty this bucket of murky water once and for all.

As you are creating your Acknowledgement list, initially it may be easier to think of negative things to acknowledge your ex for. Truth be told, you've probably done that already and as you can see, the positive results you get from making your ex wrong are zero to none. Why? Because on a deeper level, you're really just making yourself wrong for loving that person and you deepen your self-doubts regarding your judgment of character. Real empowerment and powerful transformative results are the bi-products of sincere and positive acknowledgments.

Whenever you acknowledge the greatness in anyone, you are acknowledging the greatness in yourself because if you can see it, somewhere you are being it. This holds true for negative things you see and positive things you see. This is also why it's crucial to your well-being that you only see and acknowledge that which is right and great. So, now from a space of all that is right and great, begin your list and know that on the other side of this process, your freedom awaits you.

Dear _____, these are the things I would like to ACKNOWLEDGE YOU for creating during our time together:

1. _____
2. _____
3. _____
4. _____
5. _____
6. _____
7. _____
8. _____
9. _____
10. _____

Dear _____ *, these are the*
things I would like you to ACKNOWLEDGE ME for
creating during our time together:

1. _____
2. _____
3. _____
4. _____
5. _____
6. _____
7. _____
8. _____
9. _____
10. _____

Having completed your acknowledgement lists, I now ask you to look and see if there is anything left for you to say to your ex. If there is something left for you to say then either write what you want to say in a letter (that you will never mail) or have a friend listen to you as you pretend that your friend is your ex. The bottom line is, after each relationship, our buckets need emptying. This cleansing process will not only assist you in getting over your ex, it will clear your bucket and make room for the bright future you will soon create. What haven't you said? What have you been meaning to say? Tell a friend. Write it down. Get it all out because it only takes one drop of murk to dirty a whole bucket of clean water. Please, use this Key to release all of that murk.

My Thoughts & Insights

You Complete You

After the game, the king and the pawn go into the same box.

-- Italian Proverb

A very good friend of mine once told me, "If you can see it, you can be it." The flip side of that is, "if you can't see it, you can't be it." What I couldn't see when I looked into my treasure chest was safety. I now understand how my exes were the mirrors reflecting the treasures of my chest back at me. They allowed me to catch a glimpse of all that I already possessed but didn't know. I now ask, if you already possessed the treasures your ex provided for you, would you still need your ex? Granted, you might still want the treasure your ex offered, but if you already possessed it, you wouldn't need it.

Wanting treasures from your romantic partner and needing treasures from your romantic partner sets the stage for two very different relationships. It's the difference between having someone who completes you or having someone who enhances you.

The challenge with compensation relationships is that your partner is completing you by offering you what you feel is missing in your life and therefore if and when the relationship ends, you will be left somewhat incomplete as a result. Alternatively, in an enhancing relationship, if and when the relationship is over, you are still left complete and you don't have to resume life with the sense of being less than whole or feeling as if something is missing.

Prior to creating and working the Keys in this book, I didn't know that experiencing myself as whole and complete was in my control. I depended on mathematical fractions to measure my experience of love. If I was alone, I could only experience fifty percent of love until a romantic partner came along and added their fifty percent to mine. Only then would we together be one hundred percent and whole. I didn't like that I could only feel complete if there was a romantic partner in my life but, again, I had no idea that there was actually an option besides living a single life as half a person.

I must admit that I became very hopeful and was thrilled, to learn that I was drawn to romantic partners because of a certain treasure. Once I knew what I was holding on to, I finally knew what I needed to let go of. However, traveling the road of *what* will inevitably lead to the path of *why*. Until I knew *why* I was holding on or hunting down a specific treasure, I couldn't promise that I wouldn't do it again. I couldn't promise that I wouldn't latch on to a new romantic partner who was dangling the same treasure in front of me. As repeating my past became more of a concern for me, I began to wonder what it would be like to be in a relationship with someone for no reason. How great it would be, I thought, if my partner showed up to the relationship whole and complete and I showed up for that same relationship whole and complete. I got inspired by the idea.

At that moment, I promised myself, before I entered into my next relationship, I would do everything I could to make sure my treasure chest was filled to the brim with safety. That very thought scared the heck out of me. I laughed. "You're such a scaredy cat, Troy!" I said out loud. Hearing those words stopped me in my tracks. I then asked myself something for the very first time. I asked myself, "Troy, how old were you when the world became such a dangerous and unsafe place for you?" Gulp. I swallowed hard. I couldn't quite locate the answer to that question but my body sensations assured me that I was onto something so I asked myself another question. "Okay, Ms. Byer, when did you first realize that the treasure you've been hunting for was missing from your treasure chest?"

In other words, "When did I realize that safety was missing in my life?" The moment I asked myself that question, tears stung my eyes and then spilled freely down my cheeks. I remembered that I hadn't felt safe since I was four years old and I auditioned for the PBS television series, Sesame Street. The memory caused me to suddenly roar with laughter. As I continued to recollect the incident, my entire dating history made all the sense in the world to me.

For my audition, all I had to do was prove that I wasn't afraid of Big Bird. No problem, I thought. Unfortunately, the red haired actor who was playing Big Bird wasn't aware that there was a child on set waiting to audition. As a result, the actor was walking around the set wearing Big Bird's body over his lower body but his human head was sticking out of Big Bird's neck. To make matters worse, he was holding Big Bird's head in his right hand like a football and Big Bird's pupils were bouncing up and down and around and around. As I stood there frozen from shock, the remorseful actor rushed towards me in a desperate attempt to comfort me. From my four-year-old perspective, all I saw was a man wearing Big Bird's body holding Big Bird's head rushing towards me. Frantic, I ran for my life! After running aimlessly in circles, I finally ran into Mr. Hooper's store and hid beneath the counter. I was waiting for someone to explain to me why Bird had a man's head.

I was suddenly relieved to hear my mother's foot-steps rushing in my direction. I was sure she would have all the answers. Following the sound of my sobs, my mother rounded the corner of the counter and dropped to her knees. I was so happy to see my mother's face until she squinted her eyes and through her gritted teeth she seethed, "You better getcha' ass back on that set girl. We need the money!" Well, I thought, who am I more afraid of now, Big Bird or my mother? Long story short, I got back on the set and I got the job. I will never forget walking out of the studio holding my mother's hand as she proudly declared, "Oh, Troy we're finally going to be rich; I love you." In that instant all I heard was "money is more important than my safety," and I also decided in that moment that my mother didn't really love me.

I then silently agreed that when I grew up, I would only love and let people love me that cared deeply about my safety. The interesting thing is that I had forgotten about this conversation I had with myself as a child. Yet, this conversation was the very conversation that influenced the design of my life. Now, here's the truth, my mother was right - we did need the money and as a result of my being on Sesame Street, we moved into a better neighborhood which enabled me to go to a better school. The sad truth is that until I was able to click with this 9th Key, the world always seemed like a dangerous place to me. Yes, my romantic choices were influenced by the fears of a four-year-old child who was terrified of Big Bird.

As I continued to work this 9th Key with every intention of completing myself by finding my treasure within, I came to realize that I didn't see safety in my treasure chest because I took it out of my chest when I was four and I kept it out. What I didn't realize until much later was if I took my treasure out of my chest then only I could put it back in because my safety was still in my hands. If we believe we have missing treasures, we get to be right about that and for sure, we will have missing treasures. If you can see yourself in an enhancing relationship, you will be in one. If you can only see yourself in a compensation relation-ship, the same holds true. Remember, everything you miss is everything you have because you cannot miss anything that you never had. Why? Because hunting for your treasures is like looking for the sunglasses that have been resting on your head like a head-band the entire time.

In a moment you will have the opportunity to say and re-create what your treasure chest is filled with as you take on completing you. At this point, you may be wondering if you really have the ability to be abundant love, financial security, adventure or whatever treasure it is you believed you didn't posses and needed your ex to provide. To address this concern if it is indeed a concern, I am one hundred percent certain that we have all been given identical boxes of crayons to creatively outline and color the life we build with our imaginations.

As you work the exercises for this Key and take the opportunity to complete yourself, I ask that you be brave and bold. If money is the treasure you've hunted for until now, really look and see if you can remember the moment you decided that you'd have to devise another plan in order to have money. If commitment or patience or unconditional love are the treasures you hunt, see if you can really get present to the last time you remember being fully committed or patient with yourself or loving unconditionally. What happened? What changed? What will it take for you to give yourself access to all these wonderful treasures again?

Exercise: WHEN DID YOU FORGET?

The treasure that I feel is missing in my life and that I've looked to my ex for is _____

_____

Without the presence of your treasure, how does the world occur for you? _____

_____

When did you first realize that your treasure was the very thing in your life that was missing for you?

_____

_____

_____

How many years ago was this incident? _____

How would you have handled the same incident if it were to happen today?

_____

_____

_____

It takes 21 days to make or break a habit. What is one daily action that you are willing to take for 21 days in order to make that treasure you found missing, real in your life again?

My Thoughts & Insights

Closure

We are literally addicted to love.
-- Dr. Young of Rutgers University

If love and cocaine are able to produce similar bio-chemical results in people, it should come as no surprise that love would activate the same neural mechanisms that are activated during the process of addiction. It is because of this that scientists have now affirmed that love is addictive.

I boldly assert that we are not really addicted to romantic love, we are addicted to self love. We are addicted to our need to experience ourselves, our treasure chests as being whole and complete and we'll do just about anything to fulfill this craving. After all, why do people do drugs like cocaine, really? Because they want to feel good in the skin they're in. Why do people pursue love from others, really? Because they want to feel worthy of love and capable of loving – this will make them feel good about themselves.

Love experienced with others and the use of substances are merely two of the many bridges that lead us to feeling good about ourselves. The most important bridge you will ever cross in search of feeling good is the bridge that always leads you back to you. This is because the most important relationship you will ever have is the one you have with yourself. As a matter of fact, if you look closely you'll see that every relationship you have, on some level is a direct reflection of the relationship you're having with yourself or you would like to have with yourself.

When you can really be for yourself all the things you'd like to have in a romantic partner, you will attract a partner who will be for you what you are for you. Stated another way, if you can first be it, you will see it. I know this may sound silly but if you want a romantic partner who will wine and dine you, then, I suggest you clean up nicely and take yourself out for a romantic dinner date. If you want a significant other who absolutely adores everything about you, you start by adoring absolutely everything about yourself first.

Life is an inside job

You unlock you. With these 9 Keys, doors leading in and out of romantic relationships can't trap you anymore. If you do choose to love again, you will be conscious of your written, verbal and even silent agreements. If you experience heartbreak again, you will know your pain is merely a beckoning for your spiritual growth. You now have the ability to find the treasures you hunt and create the labels that work for you. You know that you are not your circumstances, your crutch or in need of being completed by another. You no longer have to carry a bucket filled to the brim with anger and resentment into your future relationships. And because you now know the boat you float, you can take great confidence in your ability to recognize a relatedness with others before agreeing to form a companion-ship.

In the magical world of love, you now possess 9 Keys that will forever empower YOU to choose who you get to be and THAT, my friend, is Freedom.

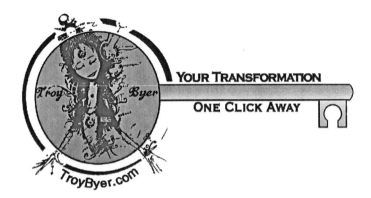

YOUR TRANSFORMATION

ONE CLICK AWAY

TroyByer.com

Troy Byer hosts the online transformational show TROY
TALKS and offers twenty-four hour support to her viewers.
Troy offers 9 empowering Keys to Freedom that can be
applied to all aspects of life. *Ex-Free* is the first in her
Freedom series books that are designed to liberate both
individuals and communities. Troy's sage advice and
inner strength comes from six years of studying ontology,
as well as her exceptional intuitive nature.

Troy Byer shares her vision in the following quote:
"I am deeply committed to being the bridge that
transforms an individual's debilitating monologues
into powerful dialogues." Troy adds, "There was a
time when that voice in my head continuously
reminded me that I was a victim of neglect, that I
was unlovable.

Then one day, something wonderful happened, I
opened my mouth and created a new conversation
about myself. When we change our conversation
about ourselves, we instantly change our experience
of ourselves. People living lives they love is what
drives me. Yeah, that's it for sure."